Cyber Security AI and ISO 42001 Standard

Mark Hayward

Published by Mark Hayward, 2025.

Table of Contents

Cyber Security AI and ISO 42001 Standard

About

    With over 23 years of experience in cyber security, this seasoned veteran of the UK Armed Forces has made significant contributions to safeguarding digital environments for local and central government departments. Their unique blend of military discipline and extensive industry expertise empowers them to distil complex concepts into accessible insights, engaging a diverse audience. As a formidable authority in the field, they are dedicated to advancing cyber security practices and promoting the ISO 42001 standard, making a lasting impact on the future of digital safety.

Table of Contents

1. Introduction to Cyber Security AI

2. Overview of ISO 42001 Standard

3. Relationship Between AI and ISO 42001

4. AI Technologies in Cyber Security

5. ISO 42001 Framework Components

6. Implementing AI within the ISO 42001 Framework

7. Challenges in Integrating AI and ISO 42001

8. Case Studies of AI in Cyber Security Solutions

9. Monitoring and Maintaining ISO 42001 Compliance

10. The Future of Cyber Security AI and ISO Standards

11. Training and Development for AI-Driven Compliance

12. Tools and Technologies Supporting ISO 42001

13. Ethical Implications of AI in Cyber Security

14. Governance and Compliance in Cyber Security AI

15. Conclusion and Next Steps

1. Introduction to Cyber Security AI

1.1. Definition and Scope of Cyber Security AI

Cyber Security AI refers to the application of artificial intelligence technologies to enhance and innovate protective measures against cyber threats. As the digital landscape evolves, the scope of Cyber Security AI has expanded significantly. This evolution encompasses various dimensions, including threat detection, response automation, and predictive analytics. The integration of AI into cybersecurity protocols allows for more robust defense mechanisms, capable of identifying and mitigating cyber risks faster and more efficiently than traditional methods. Effectively, Cyber Security AI bridges the gap between an increasingly complex digital environment and the necessity for advanced security solutions.

AI's applications in cybersecurity are diverse and pivotal. Automated systems can analyze vast amounts of data in real-time, sorting through network traffic to identify anomalies that may signify a breach. Machine learning algorithms enhance these systems by learning from past incidents, which allows them to continuously improve their detection capabilities. Moreover, AI-driven predictive analytics can forecast potential vulnerabilities, enabling organizations to implement proactive measures before threats materialize. Additionally, AI tools can assist in incident response by automating threat assessment and remediation processes, thereby minimizing the window of exposure during a cyber event.

As Cyber Security AI continues to refine its methodologies and applications, professionals in the field are encouraged to stay informed of emerging technologies and methodologies. Engaging with recent research and participating in professional networks can provide insights into innovative practices. Understanding AI's role in cybersecurity is not just about adopting new technologies; it's also about integrating these tools into existing frameworks to enhance overall security strategy. Familiarity with standards such as ISO 42001 can further empower cyber security professionals to implement AI solutions effectively and responsibly, ensuring a resilient defense against the ever-evolving threat landscape.

1.2. Importance of AI in Cyber Security

Artificial Intelligence plays a critical role in modern cyber security by enhancing the ability to detect and mitigate threats effectively. Traditional security measures, while necessary, often struggle to keep up with the speed and sophistication of cyber adversaries. AI technologies, particularly machine learning, can analyze vast amounts of data in real-time, identifying patterns and anomalies that might suggest a cyber attack. The ability to process and learn from this data enables AI systems to adapt to new threats dynamically, making them invaluable tools for organizations looking to strengthen their defence's. By automating the detection of suspicious activities, AI not only reduces the workload on human analysts but also improves the speed and precision with which threats can be identified and addressed.

Several case studies highlight the effectiveness of AI in real-world cyber security scenarios. For instance, a notable implementation of AI was seen in a financial institution that faced an increasing number of fraud cases. By deploying an AI-driven system, the institution was able to analyze transaction data in real-time and flag potentially fraudulent activities based on behavioural patterns that deviated from established norms. This proactive approach allowed the organization to prevent significant financial losses and enhance customer trust. Another example can be found in the healthcare sector, where hospitals have started to use AI to monitor patient data for signs of cyber breaches. In one case, an AI system was able to detect unauthorized access attempts within minutes, alerting security teams before any sensitive information could be compromised.

As cyber threats continue to evolve, integrating AI into cybersecurity strategies will be essential. Professionals in this field should consider embracing AI tools not just as an enhancement to their existing security measures, but as a core component of their overall strategy. Staying informed about the latest advancements in AI technologies and incorporating them into incident response plans can significantly bolster an organization's defense against cyber threats. Regular training on AI systems can also empower security teams to utilize these tools effectively, ensuring the best possible outcomes in the face of increasing cyber risks.

1.3. Current Trends in Cyber Security AI

Emerging trends in cyber security are increasingly focused on leveraging predictive analytics and automated incident response capabilities. Predictive analytics utilizes historical data and advanced algorithms to predict potential security breaches before they occur. By analyzing patterns and correlating vast amounts of information, organizations can identify likely threats and vulnerabilities that may be exploited in the future. This proactive approach not only enhances the security posture but also allows teams to allocate resources more effectively, minimizing exposure to potential risks. Automated incident response tools are taking this a step further by enabling systems to respond to security incidents in real time without human intervention. These tools can quickly assess anomalies, isolate affected systems, and implement predefined mitigation strategies. As a result, organizations are able to recover swiftly from attacks while reducing the impact of human error and increasing overall efficiency.

The advancements in machine learning and artificial intelligence are transforming future security protocols. Machine learning algorithms are now capable of evolving and adapting to new threats as they emerge, which is crucial given the ever-changing landscape of cyber threats. By continuously learning from data, AI can detect unusual patterns or behaviours in network traffic that may indicate a breach or unauthorized access. Moreover, AI-driven tools can prioritize threats based on severity and impact, allowing security professionals to focus their attention on the most critical issues first. This shift not only improves response times but also significantly enhances the decision-making process in security operations. As these technologies progress, it is essential for cyber security professionals to integrate AI considerations into their security frameworks, aligning with international standards like ISO 42001 to ensure comprehensive risk management strategies.

Keeping abreast of these advancements is essential for cyber security professionals. Engaging in continuous education and training will help develop a deeper understanding of AI and machine learning applications in security, ensuring organizations remain resilient against evolving threats. Staying informed and adaptable allows professionals to harness these technologies effectively, ultimately fortifying their cybersecurity strategies.

2. Overview of ISO 42001 Standard

2.1. Historical Context of ISO Standards

The development of ISO standards began in the aftermath of World War II, a time when nations recognized the need for international cooperation to facilitate trade and improve quality in various sectors. The International Organization for Standardization (ISO) was established in 1947 to create a global framework that would enhance efficiency and safety across products and services. Through the years, ISO standards have become instrumental in establishing global best practices, especially in manufacturing and management systems. These standards have not only helped organizations gain credibility and improve product quality but have also fostered competitive advantage in a rapidly globalizing marketplace. As businesses began to operate internationally, the need for standardized protocols became imperative for effective communication, risk management, and operational consistency.

The rapid evolution of technology in recent decades has also prompted the emergence of specialized standards, particularly in the realm of cybersecurity. Cybersecurity threats have burgeoned with increased digitization and internet connectivity, leading to the formulation of dedicated cybersecurity standards that respond to these challenges. The introduction of standards such as ISO/IEC 27001 has marked a significant step towards establishing a structured approach to managing sensitive information. These standards reflect a moving target, adapting to new threats and vulnerabilities in the technological landscape. For instance, with the rise of cloud computing, mobile devices, and IoT (Internet of Things), cybersecurity standards must continuously evolve to address the complexities introduced by these technologies. Hence, cybersecurity standards serve not only as guidelines but also as a benchmark for organizations striving to safeguard their data and infrastructure against relentless cyber threats.

Awareness of ISO standards, particularly in the context of cybersecurity, is becoming increasingly vital for professionals in the field. The ISO 42001 standard on AI governance represents a new frontier where cybersecurity and artificial intelligence intersect. Understanding this standard will be critical for organizations looking to integrate AI technologies into their operations securely and responsibly. Cybersecurity professionals must familiarize themselves with such standards to effectively manage risks associated with AI and ensure compliance while fostering innovation in their respective organizations. Recognizing the historical context of these standards can provide valuable insights into their significance and the role they play in shaping future practices in cybersecurity.

2.2. Key Objectives of ISO 42001

The primary objectives of the ISO 42001 standard focus on establishing a framework for the implementation of artificial intelligence in cybersecurity. This standard recognizes the growing role of AI in mitigating risks associated with cyber threats and aims to create guidelines that promote secure and responsible use of AI technologies within organizations. By setting clear benchmarks for ethical AI deployment, ISO 42001 addresses issues such as transparency, accountability, and bias, which are crucial for maintaining trust in AI systems. It encourages organizations to adopt best practices that not only enhance their security posture but also align with legal and ethical standards in handling sensitive data. Additionally, the standard fosters collaboration among stakeholders, ensuring that the deployment of AI is consistent and effective across various domains, ultimately leading to more resilient cybersecurity strategies.

ISO 42001 also places significant emphasis on enhancing organizational resilience in the face of evolving cyber threats. The standard outlines a holistic approach that integrates AI technologies into existing cybersecurity frameworks, allowing organizations to anticipate, detect, and respond to threats more effectively. By leveraging AI's capabilities for real-time analysis and threat intelligence, organizations can improve their incident response times and minimize the potential impact of cyber incidents. Furthermore, ISO 42001 promotes continuous improvement and adaptive learning, encouraging organizations to regularly update their AI systems and cybersecurity measures in response to emerging threats. This proactive stance not only reinforces an organization's defence's but also cultivates a culture of security where employees are trained to recognize and address vulnerabilities.

Understanding the objectives of ISO 42001 is vital for cybersecurity professionals who wish to leverage AI effectively. Familiarity with the standards can provide valuable insights into implementing AI solutions that not only enhance security measures but also contribute to a resilient infrastructure. As cyber threats continue to evolve, integrating the principles of ISO 42001 into everyday practices is an essential step towards safeguarding organizational assets and maintaining a competitive edge in the digital landscape. Adopting these standards will empower professionals to navigate the complexities of AI in cybersecurity confidently.

2.3. Benefits of Implementing ISO 42001

Aligning with ISO 42001 offers numerous advantages, particularly in the realm of risk management and compliance. By adhering to this standard, organizations can systematically identify and evaluate cybersecurity risks, leading to more informed decision-making. ISO 42001 promotes a proactive approach to risk management, allowing organizations to implement necessary controls and measures before vulnerabilities can be exploited. This not only enhances the overall security posture but also builds a framework for compliance with various legal and regulatory requirements, reducing the likelihood of penalties or legal issues. Improved risk management fosters a culture of continuous monitoring and assessment, enabling teams to be agile in responding to emerging threats. Consequently, organizations can confidently demonstrate their commitment to cybersecurity, which in turn can enhance stakeholder trust and reputation.

In terms of strategic benefits, adopting ISO 42001 places organizations at a significant advantage in their cybersecurity practices. By integrating this standard, entities can align their cybersecurity strategies with broader business goals, ensuring that security considerations are woven into every layer of operations. This alignment enhances collaboration between teams, as it encourages a unified approach to tackling cybersecurity challenges. Firms that embrace ISO 42001 often find improved communication and coordination both internally and externally, leading to faster incident response times and a better return on investment in security technologies. Furthermore, aligning with a recognized standard like ISO 42001 can elevate an organization's competitive edge, making it more attractive to clients and partners who prioritize security assurance. Additionally, the clarity and rigor that comes with the standard can aid in training and developing staff, equipping them with the knowledge necessary to navigate the complex landscape of cybersecurity.

Organizations looking to implement ISO 42001 should consider conducting a thorough gap analysis to identify current strengths and weaknesses in their cybersecurity measures. This practical step can provide insights into areas for improvement and help prioritize actions for compliance with the standard. Engaging stakeholders from various departments during this process can foster a sense of ownership and collaboration, essential for the successful integration of ISO 42001 into existing practices.

3. Relationship Between AI and ISO 42001

3.1. Integration of AI in Compliance Processes

Organizations striving to achieve compliance with ISO 42001 standards can significantly benefit from the integration of artificial intelligence into their processes. AI technologies can analyze vast amounts of data to identify gaps and areas of non-compliance more efficiently than traditional methods. By utilizing machine learning algorithms, businesses can automate the tedious and often error-prone tasks associated with compliance checks. These systems can help in predicting compliance risks based on historical data, enabling organizations to address potential issues before they escalate. Furthermore, AI can streamline the documentation process by automatically generating required reports, thus allowing compliance teams to focus on strategic activities rather than getting bogged down in administrative work.

Automation is key to enhancing monitoring and reporting tasks in the compliance landscape. By implementing AI-driven solutions, organizations can monitor compliance metrics in real-time, ensuring that any deviations are detected as soon as they occur. This level of proactive oversight not only improves response times but also fosters a culture of compliance within the organization. Automated reporting tools can sift through data and compile comprehensive reports that meet ISO 42001 standards without heavy manual intervention. Such tools can vastly improve the accuracy and timeliness of reporting, allowing cybersecurity professionals to present clearer insights into compliance statuses and risks to stakeholders.

Understanding the capabilities of AI in these areas is crucial for cybersecurity professionals aiming to drive compliance efforts effectively. Leveraging AI tools not only provides a competitive edge but also aligns with best practices in data governance and risk management. As these technologies evolve, cybersecurity experts should stay informed and consider how AI can be a game-changer in achieving and maintaining compliance with standard regulatory frameworks.

3.2. AI's Role in Risk Management According to ISO 42001

AI technologies offer powerful tools for transforming risk assessment and mitigation processes, enabling organizations to identify potential vulnerabilities and threats more efficiently. By analyzing vast amounts of data, AI can discern patterns and trends that may escape human analysts, allowing for a more proactive approach. For instance, machine learning algorithms can evaluate historical incidents and predict future risks based on emerging behaviours and developments. These capabilities enhance the accuracy of risk assessments and provide actionable insights for mitigating risks before they manifest into larger issues. Furthermore, natural language processing can be utilized to sift through unstructured data, such as reports and social media feeds, helping organizations to stay informed about potential risks stemming from external environments.

Integrating AI tools within the framework of ISO 42001 streamlines the production of risk management reports that meet the standard's rigorous requirements. AI can automate the aggregation and analysis of data, ensuring that reports are not only timely but also rich in relevant content. This means cybersecurity professionals can focus more on strategic decisions rather than getting bogged down by manual data collection. By employing AI, organizations can generate insights that align with ISO requirements, leading to enhanced compliance and governance. Moreover, the use of AI-driven dashboards enables stakeholders to visualize risks and trends effectively, facilitating better communication and decision-making. Emphasizing transparency, AI tools contribute to a thorough documentation process that supports compliance and demonstrates an organization's commitment to effective risk management.

To maximize the benefits of AI in risk management, it is crucial for cybersecurity professionals to foster collaboration between AI technologies and human expertise. Regular training and updates on AI capabilities will ensure that professionals can interpret and act on AI-generated insights effectively. By maintaining a human-in-the-loop approach, organizations can enhance their risk management strategies while remaining agile in the face of evolving threats.

3.3. Enhancing Security Controls with AI Techniques

Artificial Intelligence (AI) techniques offer powerful ways to enhance existing security controls in cyber environments. Traditional security systems often rely on fixed rules and patterns to identify threats, which can leave organizations vulnerable to new and evolving attacks. By integrating AI, specifically machine learning algorithms and deep learning models, security frameworks can gain an adaptive edge. For instance, AI systems can analyze vast amounts of data in real-time, learning from past incidents to identify anomalies that deviate from established user behaviour patterns. This means that rather than merely reacting to threats, AI can proactively predict and mitigate potential risks before they escalate. Techniques such as natural language processing allow security tools to understand and anticipate malicious intent in human language, helping to filter out phishing attempts and other social engineering attacks more effectively.

Numerous examples illustrate how AI applications enhance threat detection and response capabilities. Security Information and Event Management (SIEM) platforms, for instance, are increasingly incorporating AI-driven analytics to sift through log data and flag potential threats based on learned behaviours. Companies are utilizing AI for automated incident responses, allowing systems to enact predetermined actions in the face of detected anomalies without human intervention, drastically reducing response times. Additionally, endpoint detection and response (EDR) solutions leverage AI to identify and isolate suspicious activities on individual devices, ensuring that threats do not propagate through the network. Case studies demonstrate that organizations employing AI-enhanced security measures have significantly reduced breach response times and increased overall detection rates, showcasing the transformational potential of these technologies in the cybersecurity landscape.

AI not only augments existing controls but also encourages organizations to rethink their security strategies. By shifting from a reactive to a proactive stance, cybersecurity professionals can leverage these technologies to create a more resilient infrastructure. Staying updated about the latest AI developments and understanding how to implement them in line with standards such as ISO 42001 can greatly benefit security postures and promote a culture of continuous improvement within organizations. Embracing AI capabilities is no longer optional but a crucial step toward robust cybersecurity.

4. AI Technologies in Cyber Security

4.1. Machine Learning and Threat Detection

Machine learning (ML) fundamentally transforms the way organizations approach the identification of potential threats. Instead of relying solely on predefined patterns and rules, ML leverages algorithms that learn from data, enabling the detection of anomalous behaviour and emerging threats in real-time. By analyzing vast quantities of data and identifying subtle patterns, machine learning algorithms can significantly enhance threat detection capabilities. This approach allows for proactive measures against cyber threats, as the systems evolve and adapt to new data, improving their efficiency over time. The principles of machine learning involve supervised, unsupervised, and reinforcement learning—each contributing to a comprehensive understanding of unusual activities that may indicate security breaches.

Successful implementations of machine learning in threat detection span various sectors, showcasing its versatility and effectiveness. In the financial sector, for instance, machine learning algorithms are employed to detect fraudulent transactions by analyzing user behaviour patterns and transaction histories. Security firms utilize ML models to monitor network traffic and identify potential intrusions based on deviations from established normal behaviour. Healthcare institutions also adopt machine learning for identifying breaches in patient data security, alerting them to unauthorized access attempts. In government and defense, ML systems are used to scan communications and social media for threats, greatly enhancing intelligence-gathering capabilities. These applications serve as powerful examples of how machine learning is reshaping threat detection and response strategies across diverse industries.

For cybersecurity professionals looking to implement AI solutions in alignment with ISO 42001 standards, understanding the specific use cases of machine learning in threat detection is crucial. Engaging with ML frameworks that prioritize data privacy and security will not only improve identification of potential threats but also ensure compliance with relevant regulations. As the landscape of cyber threats continually evolves, remaining informed about the latest machine learning advancements will be essential for effective threat detection. Consider exploring robust ML tools designed for your specific sector, and focus on continuous training of these models to keep up with new types of attacks and vulnerabilities.

4.2. Natural Language Processing in Security Analysis

Natural language processing (NLP) plays a vital role in analyzing security-related textual data by transforming large volumes of unstructured information into actionable insights. Security professionals often grapple with an overwhelming amount of threat data generated from various sources, including social media, news outlets, and internal communication logs. By utilizing NLP techniques, cybersecurity experts can extract relevant information from these sources effectively. For instance, sentiment analysis helps in gauging public opinion regarding specific threats, while entity recognition can identify organizations, individuals, or technologies mentioned in a given dataset. These tools allow analysts to prioritize threats based on their contextual relevance and potential impact.

Assessing the effectiveness of NLP in enhancing threat intelligence gathering reveals that it significantly accelerates the identification of emerging threats. Traditional methods often involve manually sifting through extensive data, which is both time-consuming and prone to human error. NLP automates the preliminary analysis, flagging key incidents or patterns that may otherwise go unnoticed. Machine learning models can further refine this process by learning from past incidents to better detect anomalies and predict potential future threats. This proactive approach not only increases efficiency but also enables organizations to respond to threats more swiftly and effectively.

The integration of NLP in security analysis is not merely about technology; it also involves establishing robust processes to interpret insights accurately. Cybersecurity professionals should consider developing clear guidelines and protocols to ensure that the outcomes derived from NLP applications are aligned with their organizational risk management strategies. Establishing metrics to measure the success of these initiatives can provide valuable feedback for continuous improvement. Ultimately, implementing NLP within security workflows fosters more informed decision-making, enhancing an organization's ability to strategically allocate resources and prioritize potential risks.

4.3. Behavioural Analytics for Cyber Defense

Behavioural analytics refers to the process of analyzing patterns in user behaviour to identify potential security threats within an organization's digital environment. Its significance lies in establishing a proactive cyber defense strategy. By understanding what constitutes normal behaviour for users and systems, cybersecurity professionals can more effectively detect deviations that may indicate malicious activity. This approach allows organizations to shift from reactive measures, which often come too late, to a proactive stance where unusual behaviour triggers alerts, enabling immediate investigation and response before a breach occurs. The emphasis on behaviour rather than solely on traditional security measures helps to fill the gaps left by signature-based detection methods, which are often ineffective against sophisticated attacks. Behavioural analytics empowers organizations to gain deeper insights into user interactions and the overall health of their systems.

AI-driven behavioural analytics brings an additional layer of sophistication to this process by harnessing machine learning algorithms to detect anomalies that could signify breaches. These AI models are trained on vast amounts of data, learning to recognize subtle patterns that human analysts might miss. For instance, if a user suddenly starts accessing sensitive files they have never touched before or logs in at unusual hours, the AI can flag this activity for further investigation. This capability is especially crucial in an era where cyber threats are increasingly complex and evolving. By continuously adapting to new data, AI systems improve their accuracy in distinguishing legitimate behaviour from potential threats, significantly reducing the time required to identify and respond to incidents. Such real-time detection not only enhances the security posture but also fosters a culture of vigilance and responsiveness across the organization.

In practical applications, integrating behavioural analytics with existing security technologies enhances an organization's overall defense strategy. Cybersecurity professionals should continuously educate themselves on the evolving landscape of AI technologies and their implementation within ISO 42001 standards. This knowledge allows them to incorporate behavioural analytics effectively, aligning their methods with global best practices while leveraging AI's capabilities to bolster their cyber defenses. An effective practical tip for organizations is to start small by focusing on specific use cases where behavioural analytics can make the most immediate impact, such as monitoring for unusual login patterns or detecting insider threats. This targeted approach helps familiarize teams with the technology, ensures better resource allocation, and sets the stage for larger-scale implementations in the future.

5. ISO 42001 Framework Components

5.1. Governance and Organizational Structure

Implementing ISO 42001 effectively requires a robust governance model that aligns with the organization's strategic objectives and risk management initiatives. This model should establish clear channels of authority and decision-making processes that facilitate proactive cybersecurity measures. Organizations must ensure that their governance framework integrates cybersecurity considerations into every level, from the board of directors to operational teams. This entails appointing cybersecurity leaders responsible for overseeing compliance with the ISO standard and ensuring that policies are aligned with best practices for cybersecurity management. A governance model should also include continuous performance evaluation mechanisms to assess the effectiveness of cybersecurity measures being implemented and to adapt strategies to evolving threats.

The roles and responsibilities defined in the ISO framework are crucial for the effective management of cybersecurity. Each member of the organization should understand their specific duties and how they contribute to the overall cybersecurity posture. Executives and board members have a responsibility to champion cybersecurity initiatives, allocate necessary resources, and foster a culture of security awareness throughout the organization. Meanwhile, IT and cybersecurity teams are tasked with implementing and maintaining the technical controls that protect sensitive data and systems. Furthermore, legal and compliance teams need to ensure adherence to regulatory requirements, while every employee is encouraged to participate actively in safeguarding organizational assets by adhering to established policies and completing mandatory training. This clear delineation of roles helps create a unified approach to cybersecurity, ultimately enhancing resilience against potential threats.

Organizations should prioritize regular training and awareness campaigns that reinforce the importance of cybersecurity responsibilities among all employees. By fostering a culture of shared ownership over cybersecurity practices, organizations can bolster their defenses against potential threats. Recognizing that effective governance and clear organizational structures are foundational to the sustainable implementation of ISO 42001 inspires confidence and promotes a proactive cybersecurity environment.

5.2. Risk Assessment Methodologies

Identifying risk assessment methods that comply with ISO 42001 standards is vital for organizations aiming to enhance their cybersecurity posture. ISO 42001 emphasizes a structured approach to risk management that incorporates both qualitative and quantitative assessments. Methods like the NIST Cybersecurity Framework, OCTAVE, and FAIR are recognized for their compatibility with ISO 42001. Each of these frameworks offers a strategic perspective on identifying, analyzing, and mitigating risks while promoting a culture of continuous improvement. Implementing these methodologies not only helps organizations meet compliance standards but also fosters a proactive stance towards emerging threats. These methods encourage comprehensive risk identification, assessment of vulnerabilities, and consideration of potential impacts, which are crucial for effective risk management.

These methodologies can significantly support AI implementations for risk management by providing a systematic approach to decision-making. Artificial Intelligence excels at processing vast amounts of data and identifying patterns that might be overlooked by human analysts. By utilizing ISO 42001-compliant frameworks, organizations can train AI systems to recognize risk factors and develop insights that inform strategic choices. For instance, employing machine learning algorithms within the NIST framework allows for real-time risk analysis and anomaly detection, enhancing the ability to respond to threats swiftly. Moreover, using these methodologies in conjunction with AI can help organizations simulate various risk scenarios, facilitating better preparedness for potential incidents. This synergistic approach not only minimizes risks but also enhances overall operational efficiency.

It's essential for cyber security professionals to continuously familiarize themselves with these methodologies and technologies. Staying abreast of updates to ISO standards and advancements in AI applications will empower professionals to adapt to the evolving landscape of cyber threats. A practical tip for integrating these methodologies into AI-driven risk management is to establish a routine of regular review and refinement of risk assessment processes. Ensuring that AI models are trained on current data and feedback can lead to more accurate risk evaluations and bolster the overall resilience of the organization against cyber threats.

5.3. Continuous Improvement Processes

Continuous improvement is crucial for organizations aiming to maintain compliance with ISO 42001, which establishes frameworks for effective Information Security Management Systems. Consistent reviews and enhancements of processes ensure that security measures adapt to evolving threats and vulnerabilities. By fostering a culture of constant assessment, organizations can identify gaps in their existing systems and respond proactively rather than reactively. This shift not only helps in maintaining compliance but also enhances the overall security posture, demonstrating a commitment to safeguarding sensitive information. Regular training and updates also empower employees to recognize and mitigate potential security risks, playing a vital role in the organization's defense strategy.

Incorporating artificial intelligence (AI) within continuous improvement processes can significantly enhance the evaluation and enhancement of cybersecurity measures. AI tools can continuously monitor systems, analyze security incidents, and provide actionable insights into potential vulnerabilities. This technology leverages vast amounts of data to identify patterns or anomalies that might go unnoticed in manual reviews. By integrating AI, organizations can automate routine evaluations, allowing cybersecurity professionals to focus on more complex threats that require human judgment. Moreover, AI algorithms can learn from past incidents, improving their predictive capabilities over time, which leads to a more proactive approach to cybersecurity. This creates an environment where the systems not only react to incidents but also adapt and improve continuously, aligning closely with ISO 42001 standards for effective risk management.

For those working with ISO 42001, implementing a robust continuous improvement process can help ensure not just compliance, but also resilience against cyber threats. Regularly engage with cybersecurity teams to refine processes, and consider adopting AI-based tools that facilitate this ongoing evaluation. By embracing a mindset of continuous improvement and leveraging advanced technologies, organizations can stay ahead in the ever-evolving landscape of cybersecurity.

6. Implementing AI within the ISO 42001 Framework

6.1. Establishing AI Use Cases

Identifying and defining use cases for artificial intelligence in cybersecurity is essential for organizations looking to enhance their security posture. It begins with a comprehensive assessment of current security challenges and vulnerabilities. Cybersecurity professionals should conduct detailed analyses to identify repetitive tasks, areas requiring real-time data processing, and functions where decision-making can be augmented through AI. These use cases should focus on enhancing threat detection and response, automating routine security operations, and improving vulnerability management. It is also crucial to engage cross-functional teams to gather insights from various departments, ensuring that the proposed AI applications align with overall business objectives and address specific security issues faced by the organization.

Aligning AI use cases with the requirements of the ISO 42001 standard is a critical step that organizations must take to ensure effective implementation of artificial intelligence systems in cybersecurity. ISO 42001 emphasizes the importance of integrating AI into organizational processes while maintaining privacy, security, and compliance. Therefore, professionals should map the identified use cases against ISO 42001 guidelines, ensuring that each application enhances data governance and risk management practices. This involves assessing how AI technologies can be developed and deployed to meet defined standards for security, accountability, and transparency. Establishing a robust framework that adheres to ISO 42001 will facilitate gaining stakeholder trust while ensuring that AI initiatives align with regulatory requirements and industry best practices.

To streamline the process of developing AI use cases in cybersecurity, organizations can start by creating a collaborative environment that encourages innovation and experimentation. This includes establishing pilot projects where AI solutions can be tested in real-world scenarios, allowing organizations to gather valuable data and insights. Moreover, maintaining open lines of communication within teams fosters a culture of continuous learning and adaptation, which is essential in the fast-evolving field of cybersecurity. Ongoing evaluation and refinement of AI use cases will help organizations not only keep pace with emerging threats but also ensure compliance with standards like ISO 42001.

6.2. Aligning AI Solutions with ISO Standards

Integrating AI solutions within the ISO framework requires a strategic approach that considers both the technical and organizational aspects of implementation. This alignment begins with understanding the key principles of ISO standards and how they relate to AI technologies. Organizations must first conduct a thorough assessment of their existing AI capabilities and identify areas where they can meet or exceed ISO requirements. Developing a clear roadmap that aligns AI initiatives with the specific guidelines of ISO 42001 is essential. It is crucial to foster a culture of compliance throughout the organization, ensuring that all stakeholders, from leadership to technical teams, understand the importance of adhering to these standards. Collaboration is another vital strategy; integrating input from various departments can facilitate a more holistic approach. Agreeing on common objectives and establishing an interdisciplinary team can help bridge gaps between AI functions and ISO standards. Additionally, investing in training for personnel involved in AI initiatives can enhance understanding and implementation of ISO standards, making the process smoother and more effective.

Even with a solid strategy, organizations often encounter common pitfalls when aligning AI initiatives with ISO standards. One major challenge is the misconception that compliance is solely the responsibility of a dedicated team. In reality, alignment should be a collective effort, requiring engagement from all employees. Another issue arises from a lack of clear communication regarding the ISO standards. If team members are unaware of these standards or do not understand their implications for AI deployment, the initiative risks falling short of compliance. Overengineering solutions can also present a problem, as teams may attempt to make AI systems overly complex in the pursuit of compliance, leading to operational inefficiencies. Lastly, failing to continuously monitor and evaluate AI systems against ISO standards can result in outdated practices that no longer meet the evolving criteria. Organizations need to establish ongoing mechanisms for review and adaptation to maintain alignment with ISO standards.

When striving for compliance with ISO 42001, one practical tip is to document every step of the process. This means keeping detailed records of how AI initiatives were developed, the rationale for decisions, and adjustments made in response to ISO guidelines. Having comprehensive documentation not only aids in demonstrating compliance but also facilitates future audits and reviews. It serves as a valuable resource for refining processes and training new personnel, thus promoting a culture of continuous improvement in alignment with standards.

6.3. Measuring AI Effectiveness in Compliance

Establishing metrics for assessing the effectiveness of AI in meeting ISO requirements is essential for organizations aiming to enhance their compliance efforts. Metrics can serve as indicators of how well AI-driven systems align with established standards like ISO 42001. For instance, organizations might measure incident response time and accuracy in detecting compliance violations. Another important metric could be the percentage of false positives generated by the AI during monitoring processes, as this can directly impact operational efficiency. Additionally, tracking the rate of identified risks that were proactively mitigated through AI recommendations also provides insight into the system's effectiveness. It's crucial to ensure that these metrics are quantifiable and directly linked to ISO compliance goals, allowing organizations to analyze performance over time and identify areas needing improvement.

Organizations can leverage these metrics for continuous improvement in multiple ways. Regularly analyzing performance against established benchmarks can help identify trends and uncover insights that may not be immediately apparent. For example, if incident response times lag behind industry standards, teams can delve deeper to ascertain the cause, whether it is an issue with data quality, algorithm tuning, or user training. Furthermore, feedback loops play a pivotal role; integrating insights from compliance assessments into AI training datasets can refine algorithms continuously. This iterative process ensures that AI tools not only meet current compliance requirements but also evolve as standards and threats change. By fostering a culture of feedback and constant learning, organizations can create a resilient compliance framework that adapts seamlessly to new challenges.

Ultimately, measuring AI effectiveness in compliance yields valuable data for making informed decisions. As organizations gather and analyze these insights, they should focus not just on compliance, but also on aligning AI initiatives with broader business objectives. A practical tip for cyber security professionals is to foster collaboration between AI developers, compliance officers, and operational teams. This cross-functional approach ensures that everyone understands the metrics and their significance, enhancing the capability of AI systems to effectively support compliance efforts.

7. Challenges in Integrating AI and ISO 42001

7.1. Technical Limitations of AI

Many technical challenges complicate the deployment of AI in cybersecurity contexts. One major issue is the quality of data. Cybersecurity relies heavily on accurate and diverse datasets. If the data used to train AI models is incomplete or biased, the resulting algorithms can produce unreliable outcomes, leading to ineffective threat detection or response. Additionally, AI models often struggle with real-time data processing. The volume and speed at which cybersecurity threats emerge can overwhelm systems, requiring advanced processing capabilities that are not universally available. Furthermore, AI systems can be vulnerable to adversarial attacks, where malicious actors exploit weaknesses in machine learning models. This type of manipulation can cause AI to misidentify threats or bypass security measures entirely.

To overcome these limitations, organizations can employ several strategies. First, enhancing dataset quality through careful selection and preprocessing can significantly improve AI performance. Implementing a feedback loop where AI systems continually learn from new data in real-time can also help adapt to evolving cyber threats. Using a hybrid approach that combines AI with human expertise can further bolster effectiveness, as human analysts can provide context and intuition that machines often lack. Investment in robust infrastructure that supports high-speed data processing will enable AI systems to operate more efficiently in real-time environments. Finally, organizations should prioritize ongoing education and training to ensure that cybersecurity professionals are equipped with the skills needed to manage and mitigate AI-related risks effectively.

Staying informed about the latest developments in AI and related cybersecurity standards, such as ISO 42001, is crucial for professionals. This awareness allows cybersecurity teams to engage with best practices and frameworks that can guide the effective integration of AI into their security strategies.

7.2. Human Factors and Resistance to Change

The adoption of AI technologies in organizations often hinges on human factors that can significantly influence success or failure. Employees may feel a sense of apprehension about AI, stemming from fears of job displacement, a lack of understanding of how these technologies will be integrated into their workflows, or even doubts about the reliability of AI systems. These feelings can lead to resistance, making it crucial for leaders to recognize the emotional and psychological barriers that employees may face. Organizations must address these concerns through effective communication, transparent processes, and appropriate training that enhances confidence in using AI technologies. Engaging employees early in the implementation process can provide them with a sense of ownership and control, which can alleviate fears and foster a more receptive environment for technological change.

Managing resistance to change requires a thoughtful and strategic approach. Creating a culture that embraces innovation begins with leadership that demonstrates a commitment to understanding employee concerns and actively working to mitigate them. Leaders should prioritize open dialogue, allowing team members to express their thoughts and feelings about AI adoption. Incorporating feedback into training programs can also ensure that employees feel heard and valued. Additionally, highlighting positive case studies where AI has enhanced productivity and efficiency can help dispel myths and build enthusiasm. Offering ongoing support, mentoring, and resources also empowers employees, encouraging them to engage with AI rather than resist it.

Promoting a culture of acceptance and innovation does not happen overnight. It requires continuous effort and reinforcement from management. Establishing clear goals for AI implementation and demonstrating how these align with the organization's mission and values can inspire employees to see themselves as part of the change rather than as outsiders. Regularly celebrating small victories during the integration process can help to maintain momentum and positivity among staff. As organizations navigate the complexities of AI technology, recognizing the importance of human factors in this journey is essential to achieving a successful transformation.

7.3. Legal and Ethical Considerations

The use of artificial intelligence (AI) in cybersecurity brings a host of legal implications, particularly concerning data protection laws. One of the primary legal frameworks that professionals must navigate is the General Data Protection Regulation (GDPR) in Europe, which sets strict guidelines on the collection and processing of personal data. AI systems often rely on vast datasets to learn and make decisions, raising concerns about how this data is gathered, used, and shared. It is essential for cybersecurity professionals to ensure that AI applications comply with these regulations to avoid heavy fines and legal repercussions. This includes obtaining explicit consent from individuals whose data is utilized, anonymizing data where possible, and developing transparent algorithms that can be audited for compliance. Additionally, organizations must consider the implications of data breaches involving AI systems, which can lead to not only significant financial loss but also damage to reputation and trust.

Ethical dilemmas emerge as AI takes on more substantial decision-making roles within security contexts. One notable issue is the potential for bias in AI algorithms, which can lead to discriminatory practices, particularly if the datasets used are not representative. Cybersecurity professionals must be vigilant about the integrity of the data input into AI systems, as this can shape outcomes in ways that are unfair or harmful. Furthermore, the use of AI for surveillance and monitoring can raise ethical questions around privacy and civil liberties. Striking a balance between the need for security and the respect for individual privacy is critical. It is vital for professionals in the field to engage in ongoing dialogues about the ethical implications of their work, consider the broader societal impact of AI technologies, and work to establish ethical guidelines that prioritize human rights while advancing technological capabilities.

Implementing AI in cybersecurity not only demands compliance with legal standards but also requires a commitment to ethical principles that transcend mere adherence to law. As professionals develop and deploy AI systems, they should integrate ethics into their operational practices. This can involve conducting ethical audits, engaging with diverse stakeholders, and fostering an organizational culture that values ethical reasoning. As the landscape of cybersecurity technologies evolves, remaining informed about both legal changes and ethical considerations will empower professionals to navigate challenges effectively while maintaining public trust and safeguarding fundamental rights.

8. Case Studies of AI in Cyber Security Solutions

8.1. Successful Implementations in Large Enterprises

Examining case studies of successful AI deployments in major corporations like IBM, Google, and Siemens reveals valuable insights for cybersecurity professionals. For instance, IBM leveraged AI to enhance its threat detection capabilities, significantly reducing the response time to potential breaches. By integrating AI into their existing security protocols, they saw a remarkable improvement in identifying anomalies and automatically reacting to threats. Similarly, Google utilized machine learning algorithms to optimize its cloud security, making proactive adjustments and ensuring that data integrity was maintained at all times. Siemens implemented AI systems to monitor industrial environments, achieving enhanced risk assessments that informed decision-making in real time. These applications underscore the effectiveness of AI in interpreting complex patterns and acting swiftly within large datasets, demonstrating that a well-executed strategy can yield significant security improvements.

Smaller organizations can draw key lessons from these implementations in larger enterprises. One of the most important takeaways is the need for a clear strategy that aligns AI deployments with overall business objectives. Companies like IBM and Google highlight that a successful implementation is not just about technology; it's about understanding organizational goals and ensuring that AI solutions fulfil those needs. Additionally, investing in continuous training for staff is crucial. Major enterprises often emphasize the importance of upskilling their cybersecurity teams to work effectively alongside AI systems, ultimately fostering a culture of collaboration between human intelligence and artificial intelligence. Smaller firms should prioritize this integration of human expertise when adopting AI technologies, ensuring their personnel are well-equipped to handle new tools and methodologies.

A further practical tip for smaller organizations is to begin with pilot programs that focus on specific areas of need within their cybersecurity framework. By initially experimenting with targeted applications, they can assess effectiveness and iteratively refine their approach before full-scale implementation. This method minimizes risk and builds internal confidence around AI capabilities. Engaging with established industry networks and seeking mentorship from larger organizations also provides invaluable guidance and reduces the learning curve associated with adopting advanced AI solutions, paving the way for successful implementations.

8.2. Lessons Learned from Failed Integrations

Analyzing case studies of AI initiatives that did not meet their objectives reveals critical insights into the complexities of integrating artificial intelligence within organizations. For instance, the much-anticipated launch of an AI-driven threat detection system in a large financial institution ended in disappointment. Initial expectations were high, based on the projected improvements in identifying and preventing fraudulent transactions. However, the system struggled to adapt to real-world anomalies, leading to numerous false positives and a substantial increase in manual reviews. This failed implementation highlights a disconnect between the technology's design and the actual operational requirements of the business. Another case involved a healthcare provider's AI that sought to optimize patient diagnosis and treatment protocols. Despite initial promises, the system was hindered by inaccurate training data, which did not reflect the patient demographics accurately. This led to significant discrepancies in recommendations, putting patient safety at risk and undermining trust in the technology. These examples underscore the need for thorough testing and validation before AI systems are fully operationalized.

Identifying the common factors that led to the failures of these initiatives aids in informing future projects. A prevalent issue is the misalignment between the AI solutions and the specific needs of the stakeholders. Many organizations rush into technology adoption without fully understanding their requirements or the nuances of AI capabilities. Insufficient training for staff who are meant to operate or interact with AI systems often exacerbates these problems, leading to a lack of proficiency and reduced system efficacy. Moreover, inadequate change management strategies can breed resistance among employees, who may feel threatened by automated systems. Additionally, a failure to consider ethical implications or bias in data sets can result in not only operational pitfalls but also reputational damage. All these factors serve as crucial reminders that successful AI integration demands a clear alignment with organizational goals, comprehensive training programs, and attentive oversight to monitor the AI's performance continuously.

As lessons from these failed integrations suggest, taking a more holistic approach is vital when embarking on AI projects. Conducting comprehensive stakeholder analyses, fostering a culture of adaptability, and ensuring robust data governance can significantly enhance the chances of success. Additionally, establishing iterative cycles of feedback and refinement will help organizations remain agile and responsive to the evolving landscape of AI technologies. By acknowledging the mistakes of the past and learning from them, cyber security professionals can better position themselves to harness AI's potential effectively while adhering to standards like ISO 42001.

8.3. Emerging Startups Leveraging AI for Compliance

Innovative startups are now at the forefront of using artificial intelligence to enhance compliance with ever-evolving cybersecurity standards. These companies are harnessing AI's capabilities to automate compliance audits, streamline processes, and reduce human error, as well as generate real-time insights into compliance-related issues. For instance, some startups employ machine learning algorithms to analyze large volumes of data across various systems, identifying vulnerabilities and ensuring adherence to regulations such as the proposed ISO 42001 standard. By doing so, they not only fortify their own security postures but also provide tools for organizations that may struggle to keep pace with compliance requirements. Their tailored solutions, which often include user-friendly dashboards and continuous monitoring capabilities, allow organizations to maintain an agile compliance framework capable of adapting to the dynamic nature of cybersecurity threats.

The approaches these startups are taking could significantly reshape the landscape of compliance methodologies in the future. Traditional compliance assessments can be time-consuming and often involve considerable manual effort, which can lead to inconsistencies. The adoption of AI introduces a paradigm shift where compliance can be treated as an ongoing process rather than a periodic activity. This shift means organizations can proactively manage compliance risks rather than merely responding to issues as they arise. By integrating AI into their compliance frameworks, businesses are likely to see enhanced collaboration between IT and compliance teams, fostering a culture of shared responsibility. Moreover, as more organizations adopt AI-driven compliance solutions, a standardization of practices may emerge, enabling businesses to benchmark their compliance efforts against best practices across industries.

Understanding the innovative strategies of these emerging startups can serve as a practical guide for cybersecurity professionals seeking to improve their own compliance practices. Engaging with these new technologies can provide insights into how automation not only increases efficiency but also builds resilience against future cybersecurity challenges. It is essential for professionals in this field to stay informed about these innovations, as they could prove pivotal in navigating the complex landscape of compliance with standards such as ISO 42001. Adopting an AI-focused mindset towards compliance may empower organizations to safeguard their data more effectively while ensuring they meet regulatory requirements seamlessly.

9. Monitoring and Maintaining ISO 42001 Compliance

9.1. Continuous Monitoring Techniques

Continuous monitoring is essential in maintaining ISO compliance, particularly as organizations navigate the complexities of security and operational standards. It acts as an ongoing assurance mechanism, ensuring that processes, procedures, and controls align with requirements set forth by the ISO framework. This proactive approach helps organizations detect deviations from expected behaviours early, facilitating quick corrective actions. By integrating continuous monitoring into their compliance strategy, organizations can better protect their assets, ensure data integrity, and maintain customer trust. It also supports a culture of accountability, where everyone is aware of compliance standards and works towards achieving them consistently.

AI-driven monitoring tools are revolutionizing the realm of ongoing compliance assessment. These tools leverage machine learning and advanced algorithms to analyze vast amounts of data in real-time. By sifting through logs, transactions, and communication patterns, they can identify anomalies that may indicate a compliance lapse or potential security threats. AI's ability to learn from historical data means these systems can continuously improve their accuracy over time, leading to more effective and efficient monitoring. Moreover, they can provide actionable insights and alerts, allowing cyber security professionals to focus on critical issues rather than being overwhelmed by an influx of data.

Incorporating AI-driven tools into compliance monitoring not only enhances effectiveness but also supports agile responses to emerging threats. Organizations can set benchmarks and automate routine checks, freeing up valuable human resources to focus on strategy and innovation rather than mundane tasks. Continuous monitoring, powered by AI, gives organizations a competitive edge, making them more resilient in the face of evolving cyber threats. As cyber security professionals, it is crucial to stay informed about these technologies and integrate them within compliance frameworks for sustained operational integrity.

9.2. Reporting and Documentation Standards

ISO 42001 establishes specific documentation requirements that organizations need to adhere to for effective compliance with AI governance. These requirements include developing a comprehensive documentation framework that captures the processes, methodologies, and standards utilized within AI operations. Organizations must ensure that they maintain accurate records of their AI systems, detailing their design, development, implementation, and operational phases. Critical documentation should include a risk assessment report that identifies potential vulnerabilities and outlines mitigation strategies. Additionally, it is essential to maintain logs of decisions made by AI algorithms, thereby providing transparency and accountability. Regular updates to these documents are necessary to reflect changes in technology and regulatory environments, ensuring that compliance is not only met but also sustained over time. Effective version control practices must be adopted to track modifications and the rationale behind them.

Creating compliance reports in alignment with ISO 42001 requires careful attention to clarity and detail. Best practices involve structuring reports to include clear objectives, methodologies, results, and implications of the findings. Reports should be concise yet comprehensive, allowing stakeholders to understand the AI governance landscape without unnecessary jargon. It is vital to include metrics that measure compliance performance, providing a quantitative basis for assessments. Engaging visual elements, such as charts and graphs, can aid in conveying complex data effectively. Furthermore, including an executive summary at the beginning of the report allows decision-makers to quickly grasp the essential points. Consistent formatting across reports enhances readability, ensuring that all reports align with organizational standards. As reporting processes evolve, it's beneficial to seek regular feedback from report users to refine and improve the documentation format and content continually.

A practical tip for maintaining compliance and effective reporting is to implement a centralized document management system. Such a system not only facilitates the organization and retrieval of documentation but also ensures that all users have access to the most recent versions of critical documents. Training staff on the importance of accuracy in documentation and reporting can significantly improve compliance outcomes and enhance the overall governance of AI systems.

9.3. Internal Audit Procedures

Internal audit processes play a crucial role in verifying adherence to ISO 42001, which focuses on establishing a systematic, risk-based approach to cybersecurity management. These audits are essential to ensure that organizations comply with the standards set forth in ISO 42001. The first step in conducting an internal audit involves planning, where auditors define the scope, objectives, and key activities to be evaluated. The planning phase should also identify the resources required for the audit, including team members, tools, and timeframes. Following the planning stage, auditors collect relevant information through interviews, document reviews, and observations to assess how well processes are aligned with ISO 42001 requirements. After collecting data, analysis takes place to identify any non-conformities or potential risks. This involves comparing the existing practices against the ISO standard benchmarks. Once the evaluation is complete, auditors prepare comprehensive reports that outline their findings, including strengths and areas that require improvement. Communicating these results effectively leads to actionable recommendations and drives the organization's continuous compliance with the cybersecurity management framework.

Artificial intelligence can significantly enhance the efficiency and effectiveness of audit outcomes. By leveraging AI technologies, auditors can analyze vast amounts of data swiftly, identifying patterns and anomalies that may indicate potential risks or compliance issues. Machine learning algorithms can be trained to recognize red flags within cybersecurity processes, allowing organizations to focus their audit efforts on areas with the highest risk. Furthermore, AI can automate repetitive tasks associated with data collection and analysis, freeing up auditors to concentrate on more critical aspects of the audit, such as strategic insight and decision-making. AI-driven tools can also facilitate continuous monitoring by providing real-time insights into adherence to ISO 42001 standards. This continuous feedback loop not only improves the audit process but also enables organizations to adopt a more proactive approach to cybersecurity compliance, addressing issues before they escalate.

For practitioners in the field, it is essential to stay updated on emerging AI technologies and how they integrate with compliance frameworks like ISO 42001. Engaging in continuous learning and participation in relevant workshops or webinars can provide insights into best practices and innovative tools that enhance audit procedures. By embracing both traditional auditing skills and modern AI solutions, cybersecurity professionals can ensure robust compliance and make informed decisions that strengthen organizational security posture.

10. The Future of Cyber Security AI and ISO Standards

10.1. Predictions for AI Advancements in Security

The landscape of cybersecurity is on the brink of transformation, primarily driven by advancements in artificial intelligence. As AI technologies evolve, we can anticipate the emergence of more sophisticated threat detection systems that leverage machine learning algorithms to identify anomalies in vast datasets with unprecedented accuracy. Future systems will likely use predictive analytics to not only recognize existing threats but also forecast potential vulnerabilities before they are exploited. The integration of AI in security protocols will shift the emphasis from reactive measures to proactive risk management, enabling organizations to build defence's that adapt alongside emerging threats.

As AI continues to advance, traditional cybersecurity practices will need to adapt significantly. The increase in automation facilitated by AI will lead to a reduction in manual monitoring tasks, allowing security teams to focus on strategic planning and incident response. However, this shift will necessitate new skill sets within cybersecurity teams, emphasizing the importance of AI literacy among professionals. Investing in training programs that cover AI fundamentals and machine learning applications will be crucial for teams to stay relevant in this evolving landscape. Moreover, businesses may increasingly rely on AI-driven decision-making tools, which will raise new challenges concerning trust and accountability in AI outputs, pushing the need for frameworks such as the ISO 42001 standard to ensure ethical and effective implementation.

To stay ahead in this rapidly changing environment, cybersecurity professionals must prioritize ongoing education in AI technologies and their practical applications. Engaging with the latest research, participating in relevant training, and building collaborative relationships with AI experts in the field will be pivotal. Staying informed about how AI can enhance security measures will help professionals not only mitigate current risks but also anticipate future challenges effectively.

10.2. Evolving Nature of ISO Standards

As technology continues to advance at an unprecedented pace, ISO standards are expected to evolve in tandem. The rapid development of artificial intelligence, machine learning, and other digital technologies necessitates an adaptive response from the International Organization for Standardization. Changes in ISO standards, such as the upcoming ISO 42001, will likely focus on integrating these technological advancements into their frameworks. This means that security measures once deemed sufficient may soon need enhancement to address new threats that arise from these emerging technologies. For instance, as AI systems become more prevalent, ISO standards may incorporate guidelines on how to secure these systems against vulnerabilities, ensuring that organizations harness AI while minimizing risks. The nature of cybersecurity threats is inherently dynamic, and standards will need to reflect the latest intelligence and best practices available in the field.

Organizations striving to remain compliant face a significant challenge as these standards evolve. Keeping up with changing compliance requirements can be daunting, particularly for cybersecurity professionals who must ensure that their systems are not only compliant but also secure against a range of potential threats. This evolution calls for a proactive approach. It is crucial for organizations to engage in continuous education and awareness of incoming updates to ISO standards. Regular assessments of internal policies and practices against evolving standards will help highlight gaps and opportunities for improvement. Furthermore, engaging with ISO working groups or attending relevant workshops can provide insights into upcoming changes and their implications. Building flexibility into the compliance process will also enable teams to adapt more quickly to these modifications, allowing them to focus on not just meeting compliance but also enhancing their overall cybersecurity posture.

Staying informed and agile is essential, and leveraging technology can facilitate this adaptation process. Companies can utilize automated tools designed for monitoring compliance statuses and assessing regulatory changes. By integrating such tools, organizations can streamline their processes, ensuring they remain in alignment with current standards while mitigating security risks more effectively. In addition to technology, fostering a culture of compliance within the organization can help cultivate awareness among employees regarding the importance of adhering to evolving standards. Training programs should emphasize the significance of compliance as part of a broader cybersecurity strategy. By maintaining vigilance and innovation, organizations can navigate the complexities of evolving ISO standards while protecting their assets and reputations effectively.

10.3. The Role of Industry Collaboration

Collaboration among industry stakeholders is essential for strengthening cybersecurity measures. The complex nature of cyber threats means that no organization can effectively safeguard itself in isolation. By sharing knowledge, expertise, and resources, companies can create a resilient network capable of fending off and responding to attacks more effectively. Industry collaboration allows stakeholders to identify vulnerabilities, understand emerging threat landscapes, and develop robust defense strategies. When organizations come together, they can pool their insights and innovations, leading to shared solutions that enhance the overall security posture of the industry. A collaborative approach fosters trust and open communication, which are vital in tackling evolving cyber threats that continuously adapt and grow in sophistication.

Initiatives that promote best practice sharing and collective advancements play a critical role in fortifying cybersecurity. Various platforms and alliances have emerged, dedicated to facilitating this exchange of information. For instance, organizations can participate in industry consortia or forums where cybersecurity professionals meet to share case studies, threat intelligence, and successful incident response strategies. These collaborative settings not only provide valuable insights but also cultivate an environment of continuous learning and adaptation. Additionally, participation in collaborative exercises, such as simulated cyberattack scenarios, enables organizations to refine their response plans and improves cross-organization communication. These initiatives bridge the gaps between different sectors, leading to the development of standardized practices that promote resilience against cyber threats across the entire industry.

Staying abreast of industry developments is crucial for cybersecurity professionals. Engaging in collaboration efforts can unlock valuable perspectives that an organization might not have access to otherwise. For tangible benefits, consider leveraging tools that enable real-time information sharing about threats and vulnerabilities among peers. These tools not only help in identifying risks more swiftly but also contribute to building a culture of collective responsibility towards cybersecurity. By prioritizing collaboration, you can enhance not only your organization's defence's but also contribute to a more secure cyber environment overall.

11. Training and Development for AI-Driven Compliance

11.1. Skills Required for Cyber Security Professionals

In the rapidly evolving landscape of cybersecurity, especially in the age of artificial intelligence, professionals must cultivate a diverse set of skills and competencies. Technical proficiency remains foundational, with a strong understanding of networks, systems, and encryption technologies being essential. Knowledge of programming languages such as Python or JavaScript can provide the coding skills necessary for developing secure applications and performing vulnerability assessments. Familiarity with security frameworks and standards, including NIST, ISO 27001, and the emerging ISO 42001 standards, is equally critical. These frameworks not only guide the implementation of security measures but also provide a structured approach to risk management, ensuring that professionals can assess and mitigate threats effectively.

Furthermore, soft skills play a vital role in the success of cybersecurity professionals. The ability to communicate complex concepts to non-technical stakeholders is crucial, particularly when advocating for necessary security investments or changes. Problem-solving skills enhance a professional's capability to identify and respond to incidents swiftly, while analytical thinking facilitates the identification of patterns and anomalies that could indicate a security breach. As the landscape continues to shift with the integration of AI technologies, maintaining a mindset of curiosity and adaptability will enable cybersecurity experts to navigate new challenges and leverage innovative solutions.

Continuous education is indispensable in an industry characterized by perpetual advancement and change. Cybersecurity professionals must actively seek out training and certification opportunities to stay current with the latest trends and threats. Engaging in workshops, webinars, and industry conferences fosters a deeper understanding of emerging technologies and methodologies, while networking with peers can provide valuable insights and support. Organizations increasingly recognize the importance of investing in their teams; thus, participating in ongoing education not only enhances individual capabilities but also strengthens the overall security posture of an organization. Committing to lifelong learning is essential for those who wish to remain relevant and effective in mitigating the evolving threats posed by cyber adversaries.

Staying abreast of industry certifications is also crucial, with many professionals pursuing credentials like CISSP, CEH, and CompTIA Security+ to validate their skills. Regularly reviewing new research articles and experimentation with new tools and technologies can further bolster a professional's expertise. It is advisable to establish a routine that incorporates continued self-assessment, reflection on personal growth, and exploration of new topics. By prioritizing education and professional development, cybersecurity experts can ensure they are well-equipped to tackle the sophisticated challenges of the AI-driven era.

11.2. Best Practices for Team Training Programs

Effective training strategies are essential for equipping teams with the necessary knowledge of artificial intelligence (AI) and compliance practices, particularly in the context of the ISO 42001 standard. One of the most impactful methods is tailored instruction that aligns closely with the specific responsibilities and tasks teams will face in their roles. This involves understanding the unique challenges that cybersecurity professionals encounter as they navigate AI integration and compliance regulations. By identifying the skills and knowledge gaps within the team, organizations can create targeted training modules that address these areas directly, ensuring that all team members gain a clear understanding of both AI technologies and their implications for cybersecurity compliance. Additionally, regular updates to the training content are crucial, as the fields of AI and compliance evolve rapidly. Incorporating current case studies and real-world scenarios ensures that the training remains relevant and impactful, fostering a culture of continuous learning.

Simulation exercises play a pivotal role in enhancing practical understanding among team members. These exercises allow participants to engage in realistic scenarios where they can apply their knowledge in a controlled environment. For instance, simulations can mimic breach attempts or compliance audits, giving teams the opportunity to practice their response strategies and decision-making processes under pressure. This hands-on approach not only builds confidence but also promotes team cohesion as members collaborate to solve problems. Furthermore, debriefing sessions following these simulations are valuable for reflecting on performance and identifying areas for improvement. By analyzing what went well and what could be improved, teams can refine their skills and strategies, ultimately becoming more adept at managing real-world challenges.

Encouraging feedback from training participants is also a crucial element in refining training programs. Establishing an open dialogue allows trainers to gather insights into the effectiveness of the training materials and to make necessary adjustments. Incorporating participant suggestions helps ensure that future programs remain aligned with their needs and real-world applications. Lastly, integrating ongoing assessments can help gauge the effectiveness of the training over time and reinforce learning. Overall, the combination of targeted content, simulation exercises, and continuous improvement mechanisms can significantly enhance a team's proficiency in AI and compliance, which ultimately contributes to a stronger security posture.

11.3. Certifications Related to AI and ISO 42001

In the rapidly evolving landscape of artificial intelligence, obtaining certifications that validate skills is becoming increasingly crucial. Numerous recognized programs focus on AI, encompassing various facets like machine learning, data analysis, and ethical AI practices. Certifications such as the Certified Artificial Intelligence Practitioner (CAIP) and the AI-900 Microsoft Azure AI Fundamentals are valuable for those looking to establish their expertise. Equally important is the certification related to ISO 42001, which provides a framework for implementing artificial intelligence within organizations while ensuring adherence to ethical guidelines and promoting responsible usage. This standard assists professionals in navigating the sensitivities of AI deployment, especially concerning compliance with regulatory expectations. Professionals can enhance their credibility and affirm their commitment to best practices by investing time and resources in obtaining these certifications.

Ultimately, possessing certifications in AI and ISO 42001 can significantly bolster a professional's career trajectory. These credentials not only serve as a benchmark for knowledge and skills but also enhance visibility and marketability in a competitive job landscape. Organizations often seek professionals with verified competencies, making such certifications a key differentiator. Furthermore, as businesses increasingly prioritize ethical AI practices, understanding ISO standards can position individuals as leaders in fostering responsible AI initiatives. This capability is invaluable as companies face heightened scrutiny from regulators and stakeholders. Those with relevant certifications may find themselves more equipped to take on leadership roles, influence AI strategy at their organizations, and contribute to shaping policies that govern AI usage.

For professionals aiming to expand their expertise, pursuing certifications in AI alongside ISO 42001 provides an avenue to stay relevant and effective in a transformative technological environment. It is advisable to remain updated on newly available certifications, as the field continues to grow and evolve. Participating in training programs and workshops can also solidify understanding while providing networking opportunities with other like-minded professionals, fostering an environment for collaboration and knowledge exchange.

12. Tools and Technologies Supporting ISO 42001

12.1. Overview of Popular Cyber Security AI Tools

Artificial intelligence has progressively become a cornerstone in enhancing cybersecurity measures across various sectors. Notably, tools such as IBM Watson for Cyber Security, Darktrace, and CrowdStrike Falcon are widely recognized for their robust capabilities in threat detection and response. IBM Watson utilizes natural language processing to delve into a vast array of data and identify patterns that humans may miss, providing security analysts with actionable insights. Darktrace's self-learning technology allows the system to understand the behaviour of users and devices, establishing a baseline of normal activity to detect anomalies in real-time. CrowdStrike Falcon combines endpoint detection with threat intelligence, enabling organizations to proactively defend against cyber threats. These AI tools are invaluable not only for their efficiency but also for their ability to predict and mitigate threats before they can escalate into significant breaches.

The functionalities of these AI tools are crucial when it comes to achieving compliance with standards such as ISO 42001. ISO 42001 emphasizes a risk-based approach to managing cybersecurity within organizations, which aligns seamlessly with the predictive and proactive nature of AI solutions. For instance, the ability of AI tools to conduct continuous monitoring and generate real-time analytics supports the ISO 42001 mandate for ongoing risk assessment and adaptation. Moreover, these tools can greatly assist in incident response planning and execution, ensuring that organizations have the infrastructure in place to address potential vulnerabilities effectively. By integrating AI tools into their cybersecurity frameworks, organizations can bolster their compliance efforts and ensure their security measures meet the evolving challenges in the cyber landscape.

When considering the implementation of AI in cybersecurity strategies, it is vital for professionals to stay updated on emerging tools and technologies in this rapidly changing field. Engaging with AI solutions not only enhances an organization's defence's but also aligns their practices with recognized standards like ISO 42001, which can lead to increased trust from clients and stakeholders. Additionally, regular training and education on these AI tools and their functionalities will empower cybersecurity teams to leverage the full potential of artificial intelligence in their operations.

12.2. Evaluation Criteria for Compliance Software

When organizations set out to select compliance software, understanding the critical evaluation criteria is essential. The scope of compliance requirements can vary significantly across industries and regulatory environments, making it imperative for organizations to choose software that aligns precisely with their specific needs. One crucial criterion is the software's ability to integrate with existing systems. Seamless integration with current IT infrastructure facilitates smooth operations and ensures data consistency. Another important factor is scalability; as organizations grow or face shifts in regulatory compliance, the software should effortlessly adapt to changing demands without requiring a complete overhaul. The level of automation provided by the software is also key. High levels of automation can enhance efficiency, allowing organizations to minimize manual tasks, reduce errors, and streamline compliance reporting processes. Additionally, organizations must ensure the software has a strong user interface that is intuitive and easy to navigate. A user-friendly design can significantly improve user adoption rates, which is critical for ongoing compliance efforts. Furthermore, the security features of the compliance software should not be overlooked. Given the sensitive nature of regulatory data, having robust security measures in place, such as encryption and role-based access controls, is paramount for protecting against potential breaches.

User feedback and industry ratings play a significant role in the selection process for compliance software. Feedback from current users can provide invaluable insights into how the software performs in real-world situations. Reviews often highlight strengths and weaknesses that are not evident in promotional materials, giving prospective buyers a more comprehensive understanding of what to expect. For instance, users might share their experiences regarding customer support, implementation challenges, or the effectiveness of particular features. Industry ratings, often aggregated from multiple user feedback sources, can serve as a quick reference to gauge the overall reputation of the software within the market. Additionally, it can be beneficial to consult peer reviews or case studies, as they can highlight how similar organizations have accomplished their compliance objectives using specific tools. Engaging with communities and forums dedicated to cybersecurity and compliance can further enrich the decision-making process, allowing professionals to learn from the experiences of peers and industry experts.

Utilizing both user feedback and industry ratings can enhance the overall selection process, making it more informed and strategic. It is essential to approach software evaluation as a comprehensive analysis that not only focuses on technical specifications but also considers real-world user experiences and market trends. By combining these insights with the previously discussed criteria, organizations can select compliance software that offers both functional support and user satisfaction, ultimately leading to improved compliance outcomes and enhanced organizational resilience.

12.3. Integration Capabilities of Current Technologies

Current AI technologies possess remarkable integration capabilities with existing infrastructure. The ability of AI systems to connect seamlessly with legacy systems, cloud environments, and various application platforms enhances functional synergy across an organization. API-driven architectures are increasingly being utilized to facilitate this process, allowing AI algorithms to communicate effectively with pre-existing tools and data repositories. For example, machine learning models can now leverage data stored within conventional databases, extracting valuable insights without the need for complex migrations. This interconnectedness is not merely advantageous but essential in creating a unified approach toward information handling, data analytics, and threat monitoring.

Seamless integration of AI technologies plays a crucial role in promoting effective compliance and enhancing security posture within organizations. When AI systems are embedded within existing processes, they can analyze activity in real-time, ensuring adherence to regulatory frameworks and internal policies. This constant vigilance allows for faster identification of potential compliance breaches, enabling proactive remediation. Furthermore, the integration of AI with existing security protocols boosts an organization's defense mechanisms. AI-driven analytics can detect anomalies and suspicious behaviour much more rapidly than traditional methods, thus minimizing vulnerabilities. By ensuring that technologies work in unison, organizations not only fortify their security measures but also streamline compliance workflows, enhancing overall governance.

As organizations implement AI technologies with an eye towards integration, it's essential for cybersecurity professionals to focus on creating interoperable systems. This entails not only leveraging the right technological solutions but also ensuring that team members are trained to work effectively within this integrated landscape. One practical piece of advice for professionals in this domain is to prioritize cybersecurity assessments when integrating AI solutions. Conducting thorough evaluations will identify potential gaps in security or compliance before they can be exploited. Adopting a mindset of continuous improvement, where both AI solutions and security frameworks are regularly updated and refined, will lead to better protection and more successful compliance in the long run.

13. Ethical Implications of AI in Cyber Security

13.1. Privacy Concerns in AI Usage

The implementation of AI systems raises significant privacy concerns that demand careful consideration. One of the foremost issues is the potential for unauthorized data collection. AI systems often require vast amounts of data to function effectively, and this data may include personal information. Without stringent controls, users' sensitive information can be inadvertently captured and misused, leading to breaches of trust and privacy violations. Moreover, the algorithmic decision-making processes of AI can inadvertently reinforce biases present in the data, raising ethical concerns about discrimination and fairness. Security professionals need to be vigilant about how AI systems gather, store, and process data to mitigate risks related to transparency and accountability.

There are several strategies that cybersecurity professionals can implement to maintain user privacy while utilizing the capabilities of AI. First, organizations should consider adopting data anonymization techniques, which can help protect individual identities while allowing AI systems to analyze trends and patterns. This approach minimizes the risk of exposing personal data during processing. Additionally, implementing robust access controls and encryption can safeguard data in transit and at rest, ensuring that only authorized personnel can access sensitive information. Regular audits and assessments of AI systems are also crucial, as these can reveal potential vulnerabilities and ensure compliance with privacy regulations. Encouraging transparency in AI operations through clear user agreements and privacy policies will foster trust and allow users to make informed decisions about their data.

Finally, engaging in continuous education about privacy standards and best practices is essential for cybersecurity professionals. Staying informed about emerging technologies and their implications on privacy can help organizations adapt their strategies effectively. Collaboration between AI developers and privacy experts can foster innovations that prioritize user privacy while still harnessing the power of AI. One practical step is to create a privacy-by-design framework while developing AI systems. This proactive approach integrates privacy considerations from the outset, ensuring that privacy is embedded into the technology rather than tacked on later.

13.2. Bias and Fairness in AI Algorithms

Bias and fairness in AI algorithms are critical issues, especially in the realm of cybersecurity. AI systems have increasingly become integral to security measures, yet they are not immune to the biases present in the data and models from which they are constructed. When these biases are unaddressed, they can lead to significant implications, such as discrimination against specific groups or the overlooking of crucial security threats. For example, an AI that has been trained predominantly on restricted demographic data may inadvertently prioritize certain types of threats over others, resulting in gaps in security coverage. These gaps could be exploited by malicious actors, putting both organizations and individuals at risk. Furthermore, biased algorithms can result in unequal responses to security incidents, where some groups are heavily monitored while others are overlooked entirely. Ensuring fairness in these systems is paramount to creating a balanced, effective cybersecurity environment that protects all users equitably.

Assessing and mitigating bias in AI security systems involves a multi-faceted approach. One crucial method is to conduct rigorous testing of algorithms using diverse and representative datasets. This testing can unveil systemic biases and enable stakeholders to understand how different inputs influence outcomes. Additionally, employing fairness metrics during the development process helps in assessing an algorithm's performance across various demographic segments. It's also essential to engage in iterative feedback loops, where insights from real-world applications inform ongoing refinements. Techniques such as re-sampling data, applying adversarial debiasing strategies, and incorporating fairness constraints into the algorithm design are effective strategies to minimize bias. Regular audits of AI systems and a commitment to transparency will empower cybersecurity professionals to maintain high standards of fairness in AI applications. Ultimately, embracing these methods can lead to more secure and equitable systems.

To ensure a holistic approach towards fairness in AI, cybersecurity professionals should also consider implementing bias training programs within their organizations. Such training not only educates staff about the implications of bias but also instils a culture of accountability and ongoing vigilance regarding fairness in AI systems. Understanding the complex interplay of bias, data integrity, and the ethical framework governing AI usage is crucial. By prioritizing these principles, professionals can contribute to building robust, fair, and secure AI systems that enhance cybersecurity while safeguarding individual rights.

13.3. Transparency in Automated Decision-Making

Understanding the significance of transparency in AI-driven decision-making, particularly within the realm of cybersecurity, is critical. As organizations increasingly rely on automated systems to analyze threats and make responses, the opacity of these systems can lead to misunderstandings, mismanagement, and potentially harmful outcomes. Transparency ensures that the processes driving these decisions are visible, understandable, and verifiable by humans. This is essential in a field where stakes are high, and the consequences of erroneous judgments can be severe. By shedding light on how algorithms interpret data and make decisions, cybersecurity professionals can better evaluate these systems' reliability and effectiveness. A transparent approach enhances the capability to audit processes, enabling professionals to identify vulnerabilities or biases that may skew decision-making.

The role of transparency extends beyond merely providing clarity; it plays a vital part in fostering trust and accountability. Users of automated decision-making systems need to have confidence that these solutions are fair and just. When people understand the rationale behind decisions—whether it's flagging a potential threat or rejecting a transaction—they are more likely to accept and support those outcomes. Transparency helps establish a sense of ownership over security measures, transforming them from abstract algorithms into relatable tools that serve organizational goals. Additionally, organizations that embrace transparent practices can hold themselves accountable for the decisions made by their automated systems. This accountability is crucial in building a cooperative environment where stakeholders feel valued and empowered to contribute to cybersecurity initiatives.

One practical tip for enhancing transparency in automated decision-making is to implement explainable AI (XAI) methodologies. By designing systems that can articulate their reasoning in human-understandable terms, organizations can demystify the decision-making process. Regularly auditing algorithms and ensuring diverse datasets are used in training can also help prevent biased outcomes, creating a more equitable environment for all stakeholders involved in cybersecurity. Furthermore, involving end-users in the design and evaluation of these systems encourages a feedback loop that continuously improves transparency and trust.

14. Governance and Compliance in Cyber Security AI

14.1. Regulatory Frameworks Affecting AI

The regulatory frameworks governing artificial intelligence (AI) usage in cybersecurity contexts are becoming increasingly complex as the technology rapidly evolves. Various countries and regions have begun implementing regulations aimed at ensuring that AI systems are secure, ethical, and beneficial. In the European Union, for example, the proposed AI Act outlines risk-based classifications for AI applications, with specific emphasis on transparent and accountable systems, particularly in areas like cybersecurity. Implementing AI in cybersecurity raises concerns about data privacy and the potential for bias in decision-making processes, making compliance with these regulations essential. Organizations must carefully assess the AI technologies they deploy, ensuring that they align with the local and international legal landscape while addressing reputational risks that could arise from non-compliance.

Compliance with these regulations entails more than simply following a checklist; it requires a strategic approach that integrates AI governance into an organization's overall cybersecurity framework. Organizations must invest in regular audits and staff training to ensure that all team members understand the implications of AI governance and the importance of adherence to these standards. This means not only reviewing existing policies but also adapting them to new technologies as they emerge. The consequences of failing to comply can range from heavy fines to loss of customer trust, making it critical for organizations to prioritize compliance. Establishing a culture of compliance can enhance an organization's reputation, making it a trusted entity among clients, partners, and regulatory bodies.

A practical tip for cybersecurity professionals is to stay updated on regulatory changes affecting AI in your industry. Regularly review the frameworks from bodies such as ISO, GDPR, and NIST, and consider engaging with industry groups to exchange knowledge and experiences related to AI compliance. Implementing regular training and workshops for your team can also foster a proactive compliance culture that is agile and responsive to regulatory developments. By doing so, organizations can not only avoid penalties but also leverage compliance as a competitive advantage in the bustling AI landscape.

14.2. Developing Governance Policies

Developing robust governance policies for cybersecurity in the realm of artificial intelligence (AI) necessitates a thorough understanding of several key components. One of the primary elements is establishing a clear vision that aligns AI initiatives with the overall cybersecurity strategy of the organization. This vision should define the scope and objectives of AI use, ensuring that all stakeholders understand the intended outcomes. Involving key personnel across various departments, such as IT, legal, compliance, and human resources, is crucial to fostering a collaborative environment where potential risks and ethical considerations are openly discussed. Moreover, ensuring adherence to relevant regulatory frameworks and standards, such as the emerging ISO 42001 for AI governance, is essential. This standard provides guidelines for maintaining transparency, accountability, and auditability in AI operations, thus promoting trust among users and stakeholders.

However, organizations often encounter significant challenges when formulating and implementing these governance policies. One major hurdle is the rapid pace of technological advancement in AI, which can outstrip existing policies and regulations. This creates a gap where outdated policies may not adequately address new risks associated with AI deployments. Additionally, organizations frequently face resistance from staff who may be unfamiliar with the complexities of AI technologies and their implications for cybersecurity. This resistance can inhibit effective communication, leading to misunderstandings about objectives and requirements. Furthermore, aligning the diverse interests of stakeholders can prove tricky, as different departments might prioritize conflicting goals, such as speed versus security. These challenges underscore the necessity for continuous training and education focused on AI and cybersecurity principles, as well as for methodologies that promote open dialogue among stakeholders.

To navigate these complexities successfully, organizations can adopt a phased approach to policy development, starting with pilot programs that allow for experimentation while minimizing risks. Regular assessments and updates to the policies based on feedback and performance metrics can help ensure that governance frameworks remain relevant and effective. Employing metrics to measure the effectiveness of policies in real-world applications can provide valuable insights into their impact, guiding further refinements. Fostering a culture that encourages transparency and open communication around AI and cybersecurity will also contribute significantly to a successful implementation of governance policies.

14.3. Stakeholder Roles in Compliance

Key stakeholders involved in ensuring compliance with ISO 42001 include senior management, compliance officers, IT staff, data protection officers, human resources, and external auditors. Senior management plays a pivotal role in establishing a culture of compliance. They are responsible for setting the strategic direction and ensuring that the necessary resources are allocated to meet the compliance requirements. Compliance officers, often experts in regulatory standards, oversee the implementation of ISO 42001, ensuring that all policies and procedures align with the standard's mandates. They serve as the point of contact for any compliance-related inquiries and are integral in communicating compliance activities across the organization.

IT staff are crucial for implementing technical solutions that align with ISO 42001, such as security controls, monitoring systems, and data management practices. They ensure that the IT infrastructure supports compliance efforts and assists in identifying vulnerabilities that might expose the organization to regulatory risks. Data protection officers focus on safeguarding sensitive information and ensuring that data handling practices comply with legal and regulatory requirements. Human resources plays a role in training employees on compliance matters, ensuring that staff are aware of their responsibilities and the importance of adhering to compliance protocols. External auditors provide an independent assessment of the compliance program, offering insights into its effectiveness and areas for improvement. Together, these stakeholders create a governance framework that not only supports compliance with ISO 42001 but promotes a culture of continuous improvement.

For effective compliance, it is essential that all stakeholders communicate openly and collaborate closely. Regular training sessions for risk management can ensure that everyone is on the same page regarding their roles and obligations. Consider developing a shared digital platform where compliance documentation and updates can be easily accessed by all relevant parties. This transparency can help mitigate risks and foster an environment where compliance becomes an integral part of the organization's operational fabric.

15. Conclusion and Next Steps

15.1. Summary of Key Insights

The journey through the discussions surrounding AI and ISO 42001 reveals several key insights that are vital for understanding and implementing these concepts effectively in cybersecurity. One of the primary takeaways is the integration of artificial intelligence into cybersecurity measures, which enhances the ability to detect and respond to threats. AI can process immense amounts of data at speeds unattainable by human analysts, allowing organizations to identify vulnerabilities and anomalies more swiftly. Furthermore, ISO 42001 provides a structured approach to managing AI's operational risks, ensuring that the deployment of AI systems adheres to consistent frameworks. This is crucial not only for enhancing security protocols but also for fostering trust in AI technologies among stakeholders, who may have concerns about bias, accountability, and transparency. Key principles from ISO 42001 focus on risk management and the continuous improvement of AI systems, which helps organizations to evolve their infrastructures in tandem with technological advancements.

These insights hold particular relevance for cybersecurity professionals, who are tasked with safeguarding sensitive data and managing operational integrity within their organizations. Understanding the interplay between AI advancements and standardization frameworks like ISO 42001 is essential for professionals looking to remain competitive in an ever-evolving threat landscape. The ability to leverage AI tools effectively while complying with established standards can significantly enhance the resilience of cybersecurity strategies. Additionally, knowledge of ISO 42001 allows professionals to better assess potential risks associated with AI implementations, thus ensuring a holistic approach to risk management and fostering a culture of continuous learning and adaptation to new threats.

Keeping abreast of these developments means cybersecurity professionals will be better equipped to address vulnerabilities collaboratively within their teams and across departments. It's beneficial to stay engaged with ongoing research and updates related to AI and ISO standards since these domains are continually advancing. As a practical tip, consider developing a working group within your organization focused on AI governance and risk management. This can serve as a proactive approach to harnessing AI's potential while aligning with the ISO 42001 framework, ultimately strengthening your security posture.

15.2. Action Plan for Implementation

Integrating artificial intelligence within the ISO 42001 framework requires a detailed action plan that aligns AI technology with the organization's overall information security management system. This begins with a comprehensive assessment of the current state of cyber-security protocols, identifying areas where AI can enhance security measures. Organizations should establish a clear vision of how AI will strengthen their security posture, focusing on risk management, data protection, and compliance with established standards. Investment in training and resources is critical, as personnel must understand both the capabilities and limitations of AI technologies. Collaboration with AI vendors can provide insights into best practices and reliable tools that can fit into the ISO 42001 framework. Developing policies that govern the use and monitoring of AI applications ensures consistent governance and accountability, thus supporting secure implementation.

To begin implementation effectively, organizations should take a phased approach. Starting with pilot projects can help in assessing AI's impact without overwhelming the existing system. It is essential to assemble a cross-functional team that includes IT security, compliance, and operational staff, ensuring that the implementation is comprehensive and considers all relevant perspectives. Effective communication of the goals and benefits of AI to all stakeholders will foster buy-in and cooperation. Furthermore, organizations should establish metrics to evaluate the success of the AI integration, focusing on both performance and security outcomes. Regular reviews and updates on the AI initiatives enable continuous improvement, ensuring that the organization adapts to evolving threats and technology landscapes.

Maintaining a focus on ethical AI practices during the implementation process is essential in securing trust among stakeholders. This includes ensuring that AI systems are transparent, explainable, and free from biases. Engaging with regulatory bodies and participating in industry forums can provide valuable insights and guidance on compliance aspects related to AI usage. By fostering a culture of security that integrates AI thoughtfully into the ISO 42001 framework, organizations can fortify their defence's against cyber threats effectively. The key is to stay adaptable and continuously learn from the implementation experience, as this adaptability will position the organization to handle future challenges in an evolving cyber environment.

15.3. Resources for Continued Learning

Various resources are available for cyber security professionals seeking to deepen their understanding of AI and the ISO 42001 standard. Essential readings might include Artificial Intelligence: A Guide for Thinking Humans by Melanie Mitchell, which provides foundational concepts in AI. Additionally, ISO/IEC 27001:2013 - A Complete Guide to the Security of Information Assets offers insights into information security standards that intersect with ISO 42001. Online platforms like Coursera and Udemy feature courses tailored to AI and cybersecurity, providing interactive learning experiences. For professionals preferring a more hands-on approach, websites such as Cybrary offer free courses that cover essential topics while also discussing the implications of AI within cybersecurity frameworks. Engaging with platforms like LinkedIn Learning can also enhance your knowledge through updated courses that address current industry trends and technologies.

Engaging with industry groups and forums is another vital avenue for ongoing education. Organizations such as ISACA and (ISC)² offer memberships that provide access to exclusive webinars, conferences, and publications. Connecting with fellow professionals on platforms like the Cyber Security Forum Initiative or even Reddit's cybersecurity subreddit allows for the exchange of ideas and experiences. These discussions can lead to valuable insights about emerging threats and best practices in AI implementation within cybersecurity. Keeping abreast of these conversations can significantly enrich one's understanding and application of AI technologies under the ISO standards.

As you seek continued learning, consider setting aside dedicated time each week to explore these resources. Consistency is key in a rapidly evolving field like cybersecurity. Following a routine of reading articles, participating in discussion forums, or enrolling in online courses will help solidify your knowledge and keep you informed about the latest developments in AI and security standards. This proactive approach ensures you remain a knowledgeable and skilled professional in the ever-changing landscape of cybersecurity.